LILLE

TRAVEL GUIDE
2023

Exploring Lille, France: A Guide to the City's Holiday Magic, Winter Sports, Festivals and Christmas season. What to See, Do, and Eat in the City

NICOLAS MENDEZ

All Right Reserved!

No Part of this book may be reproduced, stored in a retrieval system, or transmitted in any form or by any means, electronic or mechanical, photocopying, recording or otherwise, without the prior written permission of the copyright owner

Copyright © Nicolas Mendez, 2023

Table Of Contents

INTRODUCTION

GETTING TO KNOW LILLE

PLANNING YOUR TRIP TO LILLE

GETTING AROUND LILLE: Your Comprehensive Guide

ACCOMMODATION IN LILLE: Finding Your Perfect Stay

SIGHTSEEING AND ATTRACTIONS IN LILLE: A Journey Through Culture and History

SHOPPING IN LILLE: DISCOVERING RETAIL DELIGHTS

DINING AND NIGHTLIFE IN LILLE: Savoring the Flavors of Northern France

CULTURAL EXPERIENCES IN LILLE: A Tapestry of Festivals, Arts, and Traditions

OUTDOOR ADVENTURES IN LILLE: Exploring Nature and Sporting Thrills

FAMILY-FRIENDLY LILLE: A Fun-Filled

Adventure for All Ages

HIDDEN GEMS OF LILLE: Unveiling Off-the-Beaten-Path Treasures

DAY TRIPS FROM LILLE: Exploring Bruges, Arras and Vimy Ridge, and the Opal Coast

PRACTICAL INFORMATION FOR YOUR LILLE ADVENTURE

LILLE ON A BUDGET: Exploring the City Without Breaking the Bank

SAMPLE ITINERARY: A Festive Winter Getaway in Lille

FESTIVE RECIPES: Cooking Up Christmas Delights

CONCLUSION

BONUS: TOP 10 MUST-VISIT CHRISTMAS ATTRACTIONS IN LILLE

INTRODUCTION

Lille, a city in northern France, welcomes visitors with its lively culture, rich history, and kind hospitality. In 2023, when you begin your adventure around this fascinating city, you'll find that it's a place where tradition and modernity coexist together. The historical importance of Lille as a commercial center and its closeness to the Belgian border have given it a distinctive personality.

In this Lille travel guide, we encourage you to stroll around Old Lille's charming streets, which are embellished with Flemish architecture, and to sample the mouthwatering French food served in quaint bistros. Enjoy Lille's colorful festivals while immersing yourself in the art and history at the Palais des Beaux-Arts. Whether you're an art enthusiast, a foodie, a history buff, or just looking for a relaxing break, Lille has plenty to offer.

With the guidance of this book, you can explore the city's beautiful lanes, find undiscovered attractions, and create lifelong memories in one of France's most alluring locales.

About Lille

Lille, which is located in northern France, is a compelling fusion of French and Flemish influences. Its history goes back many centuries since it used to be a significant commercial center, which enriched its culture and architecture. The lovely setting for your journey is provided by the Flemish and French architectural treasures that line Lille's attractive streets.

Lille, however, is a bustling hub of modernity as well as a city steeped in history. The inhabitants, referred to as "Lillois," are kind and proud of their history. The several colleges in the city give it a young attitude that gives it vitality and a dynamic vibe. Lille offers something unique to offer, whether you're an art aficionado, a gourmet, a history buff, or just a visitor looking for a relaxing break.

Why visit Lille in 2023

Although Lille has always been a delightful location, there are some specific reasons why 2023 is a great year to visit.

1. **The Fantastic Odyssey of Lille** 3000 Lille will continue to offer outstanding cultural events in 2023. A "Fantastic

Odyssey" that will immerse you in a world of art, culture, and creativity is promised by the famous Lille 3000 festival series. You may anticipate breathtaking displays, energetic parades, and public performances that will capture your mind.

2. **Historical Importance**: The history of Lille is woven together by conflicts, cultural exchanges, and tenacity. Visit the city's historical landmarks, which provide intriguing insights into its history. Examples include the Hospice Comtesse and the Lille Citadel. The conclusion of World War I will be commemorated 100 years from now in 2023, and Lille was a key player in this fight. Ongoing celebrations and festivities are anticipated all year long.

3. **Delectable Cuisine:** Don't miss out on Lille's delectable cuisine. Enjoy authentic Flemish-influenced French food. A hearty beef stew made with beer is the famous "carbonnade flamande," so give it a try. Lille is renowned for its cheese and waffles as well, providing a great culinary experience.

4. **Unique Shopping:** From neighborhood markets to upscale stores, Lille offers a variety of shopping opportunities. For a flavor of everyday living, stop into Wazemmes Market or browse the quaint stores in Old Lille.

You may purchase unique artifacts and souvenirs with a centennial theme in 2023 to mark the conclusion of World War I.

Travel Tips

In 2023, keep these helpful travel suggestions in mind to make the most of your trip to Lille:

1. **Best Time to Visit**: Lille has frigid winters and warm summers. The greatest time to go is from May to September, from late spring to early fall, when the weather is ideal for exploring and outdoor sports.

2. **Visa and Entry Requirements**: Before visiting France, find out whether you need a visa for your country. Make sure your passport is still valid for the whole time you will be there.

3. **Spending**: In general, travelers find Lille to be reasonably priced. But it's a good idea to make a budget and understand what you spend each day. The cost of lodging, meals, and activities might vary.

4. **Accessibility**: Lille is readily accessible from major European cities because of its excellent rail connections. It is simple to explore the city thanks to its effective public transit system, which includes buses and a metro. For access to several sites and limitless public transit, think about buying a Lille City Pass.

5. The official language is French, although English is widely used among the populace, particularly in the tourist industry. A few fundamental French phrases might improve your experience.

6. **Security and Health**: Travelers may feel comfortable in Lille, but it's best to follow the usual safety and health measures. Make sure you are covered by travel insurance, and learn the local emergency phone numbers. In the event of a medical emergency, the city possesses cutting-edge healthcare services.

7. **Local Customs**: The French value courtesy and good manners. It is common to extend a "Bonjour" (good morning) or "Bonsoir" (good evening) greeting. Tipping is customary, and 10% is the typical amount at restaurants.

8. **Money**: The Euro (EUR) is the official currency of Lille and France. Although credit and debit cards are commonly used, it's always a good idea to have some cash on hand for smaller purchases.

Lille beckons in 2023 with a remarkable fusion of festivals, culture, and history. Your trip to Lille is sure to be a remarkable experience, whether you're captivated by the cultural extravaganzas of Lille 3000, the city's rich historical past, or the wonderful food. Make plans, explore, and fully immerse oneself in this magical city to make lifelong memories.

GETTING TO KNOW LILLE

Lille is a gem in the crown of northern France, a city with a rich history and diverse culture. Investigating Lille's past, learning about its geography, and experiencing the distinctive tastes of its regional cuisine are the best ways to come to terms with the city.

Culture and History

The history of Lille is a tapestry made of many different influences, reflecting its advantageous position close to the Belgian border. The city, which was established in the eleventh century, has had its fair share of invasions and battles. Before becoming a French city, it was once a part of the County of Flanders and the Duchy of Burgundy.

The architecture of Lille, which has a tasteful fusion of French and Flemish styles, bears the imprint of this illustrious history. Vieux-Lille, Lille's charming Old Quarter, is home to many well-preserved Flemish-influenced structures with characteristic gables and elaborate façade.

During the Industrial Revolution, Lille played a crucial role and developed into a bustling industrial center. Due to its well-known textile sector, the city saw an inflow of employees from many areas. The robust and hospitable personality of the Lillois people was shaped by this period, leaving an enduring impression on the city's culture and character.

The two World Wars had a significant impact on Lille at the turn of the 20th century. The city experienced both death and rebirth, rising stronger after each event. It is a location where memorials and remembrances serve as symbols of the sacrifices made during these trying times.

In 2023, Lille will commemorate the 100th anniversary of the conclusion of World War I, giving tourists a rare chance to learn about its involvement in the conflict and take part in related activities. A historical destination not to be missed is the Citadel of Lille, a star-shaped stronghold constructed by renowned military architect Vauban. It served as a military bastion throughout the two world wars and is still a representation of the city's tenacity.

A dynamic blend of French and Flemish customs may be seen in Lille. Charles de Gaulle, a famous novelist, was born there, and it has a strong arts and music scene. There are several theaters, galleries, and cultural centers throughout the city where a variety of creative events and exhibits are held.

Geography and Climate

Lille, a city in the Hauts-de-France region of France, is a significant cultural and economic center due to its advantageous position at the crossroads of Europe. Its everyday life and culture have been significantly impacted by its closeness to Belgium and the Netherlands.

The Deûle River, which traditionally played a significant role in commerce and transportation, passes beside the city. Lille is a great place to start exploring the area since it is linked to other significant European cities. From Paris, it takes around an hour by rail, and the Belgian border is just a short drive away.

The sea effect on Lille's climate is what makes it distinctive. It has temperate summers and cold, perhaps frigid, winters. The greatest season to go is from late spring to early fall, from May to September when the weather is ideal for exploring and outdoor activities. Winters may be rainy, so if you're planning a trip around this time, be ready for cooler weather.

Local Cuisine and Dining

The delectable cuisine of Lille is a delightful representation of its French and Flemish roots. The city provides a wide variety of foods, each with its distinctive taste and history.

A regional specialty, carbonnade flamande is a robust beef stew made with beer and caramelized onions. For anyone looking for a taste of authentic Lille food, it is a must-try.

Moules-Frites: In Lille, mussels and French fries are a well-liked dish. Many restaurants serve this traditional dish with a variety of sauces and spices.

Waterzooi, a popular Flemish dish in Lille, is a thick soup or stew that is often cooked with chicken or fish.

Cheese: Lille is located in the center of the world's cheese area, where you can find a large selection of local cheeses. A popular cheese in the area is Marseilles, a cow's milk cheese with a pungent aroma.

Waffles: The city offers Belgian-style waffles that will satisfy your sweet craving. You may get these delectable delicacies at bakeries and cafés.

Lille offers a fantastic dining experience. Charming bistros and eateries serving both classic and modern French cuisine can be found in abundance in Old Lille. Discover the variety of restaurants on Rue de la Monnaie and have a leisurely supper on the cobblestone streets.

Lille provides a wide international cuisine scene in addition to these regional specialties, reflecting its cosmopolitan environment. There are several eating alternatives, ranging from Moroccan tagines to Japanese sushi.

The vibrant street markets in Lille are well-known for allowing visitors to taste the fruits, cheeses, and delicacies of the area. For a genuine experience, go to Wazemmes Market. The market's vibrant vendors and buzzing ambiance provide visitors with a picture of daily life in Lille.

You'll learn as you explore Lille's culinary scene that food is more than just fuel for the body; it's also a window into the city's rich history and culture.

Knowing Lille is a fascinating journey through geography, time, and the gastronomic pleasures of a city that has been molded by history and is open to the world. Lille, which blends Flemish and French traditions, provides a distinct cultural experience that entices visitors to explore its numerous treasures.

PLANNING YOUR TRIP TO LILLE

The idea of traveling to Lille in 2023 is intriguing. A vacation must be carefully planned out to go well and be pleasurable. The timing of your trip, the necessary documents to enter the country, and the expense of your trip are all covered in this section.

When to Visit

The best time to visit Lille is very important since it may greatly affect your experience. Lille has four unique seasons, each of which has its allure.

During the spring, from **March to May,** Lille is at its most beautiful. The temperature is rising, and the city's parks and gardens are awash in vibrant blossoms. During this time of year, it is comfortable to visit outdoor sites. Additionally, if you want to avoid a lot of people, this is a great time to go.

Summer (June to August): Lille has its busiest travel period in the summer. The temperature is nice, averaging between 17°C and 22°C (63°F and 72°F). Outdoor activities, festivals, and events are at their finest now. Be prepared, nevertheless, for more crowds, particularly during the Lille 3000 and other summertime events.

Early fall is another excellent season to visit Lille **(September to November)**. It is still a lovely day, making sightseeing possible. You may explore the city's attractions without waiting in line or encountering high foot traffic as the crowds begin to disperse. Particularly in September, there might be a perfect balance between nice weather and fewer visitors.

Winter (December to February): The winters in Lille are cool, with daily highs and lows between 3°C and 6°C (37°F and 43°F). Visit Lille during the holiday season if you like Christmas markets and the spirit of the season. The city is transformed into a winter wonderland, complete with marketplaces that are exquisitely adorned and an enchanting ambiance.

Entry Requirements and Visas

It's important to be aware of the admission criteria, which vary based on your country and length of stay, before starting your trip to Lille.

Lille is a member of the Schengen Area, a collection of European nations that have done away with passport checks at its shared borders. If you are a citizen of a Schengen member nation, you may visit Lille visa-free and remain there for up to 90 days within a 180-day window.

Non-Schengen Visa Holders: To visit Lille, you may require a Schengen Visa if you are not a citizen of a Schengen member nation. Depending on your nationality, certain conditions must be met to receive a Schengen visa. In general, you'll need a current passport, a completed visa application form, travel insurance, proof of lodging, and evidence that you have enough money to cover your stay.

The particular visa requirements for your country of residency must be verified since they are subject to change. The French consulate or embassy in your country is a trustworthy resource for information about visa applications and specifications. Since processing periods might vary, make sure to apply for your visa well in advance of the dates you want to visit.

Budgeting and Costs

Particularly when contrasted to places like Paris, Lille is renowned for being a reasonably priced vacation destination in France. To make sure you remain within your budget, it's crucial to comprehend the expenditures involved with your vacation.

Accommodations: The price of lodging in Lille may vary significantly. Hostels that are affordable, mid-range hotels, and opulent accommodations are all available. A mid-range hotel will typically cost you between €70 and €150 per night. Hostels may be found for as low as €20 to €40 per night if you're seeking for more affordable choices.

Dining: Eating is a wonderful experience in Lille. The price of eating out at restaurants may vary substantially. In a mid-range restaurant, a three-course dinner normally costs between €25 and €40 per person. However, you may find inexpensive meal alternatives in neighborhood brasseries and bistros. Markets and street food provide inexpensive options.

Transportation: Lille boasts a bus and metro system that is both effective and reasonably priced. One bus or metro ticket typically costs €1.60. For access to several sites and limitless public transit, think about buying a Lille City Pass. Expect to spend roughly €10 for a short city trip if you want to use a cab.

Activities & Sightseeing: A lot of Lille's attractions have affordable prices. Typically, museum and gallery entrance fees vary from €5 to €10. The Lille City Passes are very affordable and provide you with cheap access to a variety of activities and transit alternatives.

Shopping: Lille has a variety of stores to choose from, including boutiques and neighborhood markets. Set a spending limit for souvenirs and retail therapy since prices may vary greatly based on your tastes.

Budgeting for unanticipated costs, such as medical crises or sudden purchases, is crucial. It's a good idea to save up a little extra money in case of situations like this one.

The Euro **(EUR)** is the currency in use in Lille. For modest purchases, make sure you have local cash on hand, although credit and debit cards are often accepted.

Overall, Lille is renowned for providing excellent value to visitors. However, your budget may change based on the lodging, food, and activity options you choose. It's a good idea to thoroughly prepare your budget and distribute money according to your goals and preferences.

In conclusion, careful preparation is essential for a fruitful and satisfying vacation to Lille. You can make the most of your trip to this attractive city in northern France by picking the best time to go, being aware of visa restrictions, and setting aside enough money. Planning beforehand can guarantee a fantastic experience whether you're seeing historical landmarks, delighting in regional food, or taking in Lille's lively culture.

GETTING AROUND LILLE: Your Comprehensive Guide

It may be exhilarating and difficult to find your way around a new city. To experience Lille's picturesque streets and dynamic culture, a range of transportation alternatives are available. Lille is known for its distinctive fusion of French and Flemish influences. To make your trip to Lille simple and pleasurable, we'll go into detail in this information about your transportation choices, public transit, and driving in Lille.

Options for Transportation

The city of Lille is well-connected and provides a variety of transportation choices to meet your requirements and tastes.

Public Transportation: The effective public transportation system in Lille serves the whole city as well as its surroundings. It consists of buses, trams, and the driverless metro system known as VAL (Véhicule Automatique Léger). The public transportation system makes it simple to get through Lille and its surrounding regions.

Walking: Lille is a city that encourages pedestrians, and many of its attractions are close to one another. The city core, which includes Old Lille (Vieux-Lille), is small enough to be easily explored on foot.

Bicycles: Lille encourages cycling, and the city is filled with bike lanes and bike-sharing programs. An entertaining and environmentally responsible way to explore Lille at your leisure is by renting a bicycle.

Taxis: If you're traveling with baggage or prefer straight point-to-point transport, taxis are an easy and quick way to move about in Lille.

Car rentals: Renting a car might be a wise decision if you want to explore Lille's surroundings. You may discover a range of automobiles to meet your requirements at Lille's many car rental providers.

Public Transport

The public transportation in Lille is a dependable and reasonably priced way to move about the city. What you should know about Lille's public transportation is as follows:

1. **Tickets and Passes**: A ticketing system is used to run Lille's public transportation system. You may buy single tickets for a single usage or choose different passes for longer visits. The Lille City Pass, available for 1, 2, or 3 days, provides unrestricted access to the metro, buses, and trams in addition to subsidized admission to several attractions.

2. **The VAL** metro system is convenient and driverless. It links important parts of the city, making commuting easy and fast. The major railway station of Lille, Gare Lille Flandres, is where the two metro lines, Line 1 (yellow) and Line 2 (red), connect.

3. **Trams**: Lille's extensive tram network connects several areas and is a great way to go to places that the metro does not directly serve. The white and blue color scheme of the trams makes them simple to see.

4. **Buses**: Lille has a robust bus system that links the city's numerous neighborhoods. Buses are a versatile mode of transportation that often service locations that are inaccessible to the metro and trams.

5. **Validating Tickets**: Check your ticket or pass before boarding a bus, tram, or metro station. At station entrances are ticket validators. Fines may apply if you don't verify your ticket.

6. **Timetables and Operation Hours**: In Lille, public transportation generally runs from roughly 5:30 AM to midnight, with condensed timetables on weekends and holidays. Checking the timetables and schedules in advance is advised, particularly if you want to travel off-peak.

Driving in Lille

If you want to explore the neighboring areas or have certain objectives in mind, driving in Lille is a practical alternative. What you should know about driving in and around Lille is as follows:

1. **Road System:** Lille is accessible by automobile from many European cities thanks to a well-maintained network

of roadways. Due to its closeness to Belgium's border, the city serves as an ideal starting point for cross-border road journeys.

2. **Car Rental**: The major railway terminals and the city center of Lille both provide car rental companies if you require one. Before renting a vehicle, make sure you have a credit card, a valid driver's license, and an understanding of the rental terms and restrictions.

3. **Traffic Regulations**: It's crucial to follow France's traffic regulations whether driving in Lille or anyplace else in the nation. The right side of the road is for driving, while the left is for overtaking. All passengers must wear seat belts, and kids must be buckled into the proper car seats.

4. **Parking**: On-street and garage parking are only a few of the alternatives available in Lille. Checking the parking rules in the area where you want to park is advised since certain sections in the city center may have limited parking zones. Pay close attention to parking meters or ticket dispensers to buy parking permits as needed.

5. **Congestion**: During rush hours, Lille, like many other cities, may face traffic congestion. Be sure to account for

traffic congestion during peak hours on weekdays when planning your trips.

6. **Tolls**: On the road from Lille to other parts of France, you can come across toll booths on the motorway. To pay for these tolls, have cash or a credit card close at hand.

7. **GPS and Maps**: When traveling around Lille and its surroundings, GPS or navigation software may be quite helpful. To assist you in finding your journey, make sure you have access to maps or a trustworthy navigation system.

8. **Environmental Zones:** Be aware that certain parts of Lille could have low-emission zones that only permit cars that adhere to a specified set of environmental criteria. It's crucial to confirm that your car complies with the regulations in these areas.

9. **Fuel**: Lille has easy access to both gasoline and diesel. Although many gas stations now take credit cards, it's always a good idea to carry extra cash with you in case of emergencies or when visiting smaller stations.

10. **Road Signs:** The road signs in Lille adhere to international standards and are often simple to comprehend.

Keep an eye out for signage pointing to surrounding towns and tourist attractions.

In conclusion, traveling about Lille is easy and pleasurable whether you choose to drive, walking, cycling, or public transportation. It's simple to visit Lille and its surroundings because of the city's small size and well-connected public transportation system. Discovering the various riches of this enchanting city in northern France will be an easy and enjoyable experience if you are aware of your alternatives and the local laws and regulations.

ACCOMMODATION IN LILLE: Finding Your Perfect Stay

Finding the ideal lodging is a crucial part of organizing a successful vacation to Lille. Lille has a range of lodging alternatives, whether you're looking for opulence, homey charm, or affordable solutions. We'll look at the best hotels, B&Bs, hostels, and guesthouses in Lille in our extensive guide to help you choose the ideal place to stay while you're there.

Top Hotels in Lille

Many upscale hotels in Lille combine opulent facilities with first-rate service. The best hotels in the area are listed below for you to take into account:

L'Hermitage Gantois, Collection of Autographs: This five-star hotel beautifully combines old-world elegance with contemporary luxury. The hotel, which is housed in a former hospice from the 15th century, oozes richness with its elaborate architecture, serene courtyard, and luxurious suites. For those looking for a luxurious, historically significant experience, The Hermitage Gantois serves as a getaway.

On the **Place de la République**, there is a classy, five-star hotel called the Hotel Carlton. It is popular among tourists looking for elegant luxury because of its traditional French charm, roomy accommodations, and excellent service.

Clarance Hotel Lille: The Clarence Hotel is a magnificent option for a private and personal encounter. In an 18th-century house, this five-star boutique hotel provides tastefully decorated rooms, a Michelin-starred restaurant, and a tranquil courtyard garden.

Grand Hotel Bellevue Lille: This four-star hotel is situated in the center of Lille and combines contemporary comfort with a dash of traditional grandeur. The Grand Hotel Bellevue offers tastefully furnished rooms, a delightful café, and a rooftop terrace with expansive city views.

The luxury Hôtel Barrière Lille, a member of the renowned Barrière group, is attached to the Casino Barrière and provides opulent accommodations, a variety of culinary choices, and a spa for leisure. It's the ideal option for tourists looking for entertainment and luxury.

This four-star hotel, **Hotel Crowne Plaza Lille - Euralille**, is close to the Euralille commercial and business center and welcomes both business and leisure guests. It provides convenient access to Lille's top attractions as well as contemporary accommodation, a fitness facility, and.

Bed and Breakfasts

Consider one of Lille's beautiful bed & breakfasts for a cozier and more private stay. These lodgings provide a unique experience and a window into local culture. The following Lille bed & breakfast establishments are noteworthy:

La Maison du Champlain is a bed & breakfast that offers a cozy and inviting ambiance right in the middle of Old Lille. The hotel offers tastefully appointed rooms as well as a sumptuous prepared breakfast every morning.

Located in a lovely Victorian mansion, Chambre d'hôtes La Merveilleuse offers tastefully furnished rooms with a blend of antique and modern furniture. Major attractions are conveniently placed close by and accessible on foot.

La Villa 30: A charming bed & breakfast in a quiet neighborhood, La Villa 30 is renowned for its cozy rooms, a tranquil garden, and a kind host who shares helpful local knowledge.

La Ferme de la Place: This bed and breakfast provides a peaceful retreat from the bustle of the city and is situated in the countryside not far from Lille. The rustic rooms are ideal for a peaceful getaway.

The beautiful bed and breakfast Le 84 Saint-Louis is located in the center of Vieux-Lille and provides comfortable rooms with a blend of modern and historical design. It's the ideal option for anyone who wants to fully experience the city's ancient atmosphere.

Guesthouses and Hostels

Hostels and guesthouses are among the affordable lodging options in Lille. These choices are ideal for tourists looking for a budget without sacrificing comfort. Some of the noteworthy options are as follows:

Gautama Hostel: This vibrant and friendly hostel in the heart of the city is a great choice for tourists on a tight budget. It's a terrific location to meet other travelers since it has a bar, a shared kitchen, and a welcoming ambiance.

Le Cercle des Voyageurs is a low-cost inn with private rooms and common facilities that is close to Lille's major railway terminals. The on-site café offers a welcoming area for unwinding and socializing with other visitors.

Youth hostel Auberge de Dear Lillie: The Auberge de Jeunesse, which offers both dorm rooms and individual rooms, is a clean and well-kept alternative if you're searching for a young hostel experience. It is close to the city's heart and has a shared kitchen and common spaces.

Le 45 Rue de la Monnaie is a guesthouse renowned for its welcoming staff and reasonably priced, spotless accommodations. It is close to the city's attractions since it is situated in Lille's historic district.

In the center of **Vieux-Lille, Ostello Bellagio** is a cozy inn with reasonably priced lodging and a warm environment. Budget and backpackers alike will love this choice.

Take into account your tastes, vacation style, and budget while selecting a hotel in Lille. Lille provides a variety of accommodations to guarantee a relaxing and delightful stay, whether you choose an opulent hotel, a welcoming bed and breakfast, or a wallet-friendly hostel. Having the ideal lodging as your base will make exploring the city's rich history, culture, and culinary attractions much more enjoyable.

SIGHTSEEING AND ATTRACTIONS IN LILLE: A Journey Through Culture and History

Lille is a city bursting with historical sites and cultural treasures, with a compelling fusion of French and Flemish influences. The Grand Place and Old Lille, the Palais des Beaux-Arts, the Lille Zoo, museums, and galleries, as well as the tranquil parks and gardens that contribute to the city's attractiveness, are just a few of the top sights and activities that await you in Lille. We'll also go over other notable sites and activities in this thorough guide.

Old Lille and Grand Place

Start your journey of Lille in the Grand Place (Place du Général de Gaulle), the city's center. Beautiful buildings, quaint cafés, and specialty stores around the perimeter of this lively area. It's the perfect spot to take in Lille's energetic vibe. The Vieille Bourse, a magnificent 17th-century structure with a unique interior courtyard, is located on the Grand Place. It is a work of art in architecture, featuring elaborately carved columns and sculptures.

Old Lille, often known as Vieux-Lille, is a charming area close to the Grand Place. Townhouses in the Flemish style, cobblestone streets, and a variety of enticing eateries define this ancient district. You'll come across secret courtyards, artisan stores, and a stunning fusion of French and Flemish architecture as you meander through its charming streets. A lovely plaza in Old Lille is the Place aux Oignons, which has a vibrant façade and lively terraces.

The impressive Notre-Dame de la Treille Cathedral is also located in Old Lille. It is a distinctive architectural jewel due to its contrasting contemporary exterior and Gothic interior. The cathedral's interior may be explored, its stained glass can be seen, and you can take an elevator to the rooftop for sweeping city views.

Palais des Beaux-Arts

The Palais des Beaux-Arts in Lille is an essential must-see for art and culture lovers. It features a sizable collection of European paintings, sculptures, decorative arts, and more as one of France's largest fine arts museums. The museum's magnificent collections, which cover European art history from the Middle Ages to the 20th century, provide a thorough overview.

In the Palais des Beaux-Arts, famous pieces by Rubens, Delacroix, Van Dyck, and Veronese are on display. There are many departments within the collection, including those for paintings, sculptures, antiquities, and graphic arts. The museum is a dynamic cultural center because of the changing temporary exhibits that provide new insights into art.

The structure itself is a marvel of beauty, with a neoclassical design and a gorgeous glass dome. It demonstrates Lille's commitment to preserving and honoring its cultural heritage.

Lille Zoo

The Lille Zoo is a lovely retreat into the world of nature, conveniently located in the center of the city. Over 450 creatures of different species, including large cats, monkeys, reptiles, and exotic birds, are housed in this family-friendly attraction. The zoo maintains a major emphasis on conservation and education, providing visitors of all ages with a fun and educational experience.

You will have the opportunity to see animals up close in well-created habitats that closely resemble their natural settings as you tour the zoo. The zoo's efforts to save endangered species and support conservation activities demonstrate its commitment to animal care and environmental education.

The Lille Zoo offers a wonderful chance to interact with animals, understand various ecosystems, and recognize the value of biodiversity. It's a fun and instructive experience that's best suited for families with young children.

Galleries and Museums

Numerous museums and galleries that each give a different viewpoint on art, history, and heritage enhance Lille's cultural environment. Here are a few illustrious organizations worth your attention:

The nearby town of **Roubaix**, just a short metro trip from Lille, is home to the La Piscine - Musée d'Art et d'Industrie André Diligent, an art museum situated in a magnificently renovated swimming pool structure. In a magnificent location, its collection includes sculptures, decorative arts, and fine arts.

Discover **Charles de Gaulle's birthplace** at Maison Natale Charles de Gaulle, one of France's most famous residents. Through its displays and artifacts, this Lille museum honors his life and work.

Located in a former hospital, the **Musée de l'Hospice Comtesse présents** Lille's past and culture. It has a variety of relics, paintings, and ornamental objects that provide light on the history of the city.

Le Tripostal is a contemporary art venue where a variety of shows including cutting-edge and experimental works by contemporary artists are shown on a rotating basis.

The **Musée d'Histoire Naturelle de Lille** is a wonderful place to visit if you're interested in natural history. It features an extensive collection of items, which includes taxidermy exhibits, minerals, and fossils.

Hospice d'Havré: A fine arts museum with a collection of paintings, sculptures, and decorative arts is housed in this magnificent 17th-century structure. The hospice's structure is a piece of art in and of itself.

Gardens and Parks

Lille's tranquil parks and gardens provide a pleasant respite from the urban clamor. In the middle of the metropolis, these green spots provide rest and recreation:

Parc de la Citadelle: This sizable park that envelops Lille's medieval Citadel provides a tranquil escape. You may take strolls, have picnics, and observe the citadel's walls.

The Jardin des Géants is a park with large plant sculptures and well-kept gardens that is close to the Porte de Paris. It's a fascinating and lovely area to discover.

Parc Matisse: This park, which bears Henri Matisse's name, is well-known for its lovely rose garden. It's a peaceful area where you can unwind and think.

Parc Barbieux is a charming park with meandering walkways, a lake, and rich vegetation that is situated in the neighboring town of Roubaix. It's ideal for a calm walk.

The lovely Jardin Vauban, which is close to the Lille Citadel, has a wide selection of flowers, plants, and sculptures. It's a lovely location for a tranquil getaway.

Lille has a variety of sights and activities to meet the interests of any tourist, whether they are interested in history, art, and culture, or just taking in the natural beauty. Your trip through history and art will take place against a mesmerizing background influenced by the city's distinctive fusion of French and Flemish traditions, which are seen in its architecture, gastronomy, and culture.

SHOPPING IN LILLE: DISCOVERING RETAIL DELIGHTS

Lille, a city famed for its thriving culture and extensive history, is also a retail mecca. Lille's retail scene offers something for everyone, from small markets selling local products and unusual treasures to beautiful shops presenting artisan crafts. In this tour, we'll dig into Lille's shopping scene and highlight the vibrant shopping areas, quaint local markets, and specialty stores that make this city a retail haven.

Local Markets

1. One of Lille's most well-known and active marketplaces is the **Wazemmes Market (Marché de Wazemmes)**. It's a lively and colorful event that's held every Tuesday, Thursday, and Sunday where you can discover a large range of things. This market provides a variety of goods, from fresh vegetables to apparel, fabrics, spices, and even antique things. Additionally, since it is well renowned for its various food vendors, it is a great spot to sample a variety of cuisines. Wazemmes Market offers a varied and diverse shopping

experience that is ideal for getting a sense of the local way of life.

2. **The Braderie de Lille**, which draws tourists from all over the globe, is Lille's most recognizable and anticipated event. It is Europe's biggest flea market, encompassing more than 100 kilometers of streets, and it takes place the first weekend in September. The Braderie is a veritable goldmine of vintage, antique, valuable, and rare objects. This event provides a spectacular shopping experience, whether you're a collector or simply looking for one-of-a-kind keepsakes.

3. **Wazemmes Flea Market**: The Wazemmes Flea Market is worthwhile to visit if you appreciate finding hidden jewels and old-fashioned treasures. It's a scaled-down version of the Braderie that takes place the first weekend of every month and concentrates on antiques, used goods, and oddities. Because of the more laid-back attitude, it's perfect for unhurried exploring.

4. **Place du Concert Market (Marché de la Place du Concert):** On Wednesdays and Sunday mornings, this quaint market is held. It is renowned for its variety of handcrafted goods, fresh food, and cheeses. You may buy a variety of artisan products as well as local foodstuffs

including cheeses, charcuterie, bread, and flowers. The Opera House serves as a background for the gorgeous location, which adds to the market's allure.

Souvenir and boutiques

1. **Boutiques in Vieux-Lille**: This historic district is a shopping paradise, with a mix of posh shops and little boutiques. Everything from designer clothing and home furnishings to high-end foods may be found here. A taste of Vieux-Lille's distinctive retail atmosphere can be seen at stores like Le Comptoir d'Eugénie, renowned for its fashionable apparel and accessories, and Le Nez en l'Air, which specializes in home products and décor.

2. **Les Galeries Lafayette** is a prominent department store with upmarket fashion brands and high-end goods that is situated in the center of Lille. It provides a vast selection of apparel, accessories, and cosmetics, making it a sanctuary for fashion fans. The store's sophisticated design and kind service enhance the high-end shopping experience.

3. **Le Furet du Nord**, one of the biggest independent bookshops in Europe, is a paradise for book enthusiasts. A large selection of books, including books in many different

languages, art books, stationery, and even vinyl recordings, are kept at this multistory bookstore. It's the ideal location for bookworming and finding one-of-a-kind gifts.

4. **Meert**: Meert is a well-known bakery with a lengthy history that dates back to the 18th century. It is well known for its waffles, which you can buy as tasty keepsakes. These delicious sweets, which capture the spirit of Lille's culinary tradition, are the perfect gift or indulgence for yourself.

Shopping Districts

1. **Euralille** is an upscale retail area in Lille that is close to the city's two major railway terminals, Gare Lille Europe and Gare Lille Flandres. The Euralille retail mall, which has a variety of shops, global brands, and eating choices, is located in this vibrant neighborhood. It's a handy location for visitors coming by rail and provides a variety of retail opportunities in one place.

2. **Rue de la Clef**: Located in the center of Old Lille, this lovely street is well-known for its chic boutiques and artisan stores. It's a lovely area to meander around and find one-of-a-kind clothing, accessories, and handicrafts. Shopping in a charming, historic environment is possible at

Rue de la Clef, which perfectly captures the essence of Old Lille.

3. **Rue de la Monnaie**: This bustling Old Lille street is full of shops, cafés, and eateries. It's a popular shopping area with a variety of high-end clothing, housewares, and locally produced goods. It's the perfect area to explore and shop at your leisure since it's filled with a variety of apparel boutiques, art galleries, and stores that specialize in local specialties.

4. Lille's main thoroughfare, **Rue Esquermoise**, is a mecca for fashion and lifestyle shops. People who are looking for luxury clothing, accessories, and specialized shops often go there. Rue Esquermoise is a lively and buzzing location to find the newest trends and one-of-a-kind things thanks to its historic architecture and a variety of shopping possibilities.

5. **Rue Solférino:** The art galleries and antique stores on this street are well-known. It is a unique retail area that appeals to collectors and art lovers. You may look through a variety of works of art, antiques, and one-of-a-kind items that provide a window into Lille's artistic and historical legacy.

Lille's shopping scene is vibrant and intriguing, with a variety of alternatives to suit all tastes and price ranges. Lille's retail environment welcomes you to experience its character and culture, whether you're looking for antiques at the Braderie, browsing the shops in Old Lille, or savoring the gastronomic treats of regional markets. To uncover treasures that will remind you of your trip to Lille, don't forget to explore this attractive city's shopping pleasures.

DINING AND NIGHTLIFE IN LILLE: Savoring the Flavors of Northern France

A gastronomic paradise is just waiting to be discovered in Lille, a city that seamlessly combines French and Flemish traditions. This guide will walk you through the extensive and varied eating and nightlife choices that make Lille a destination for food and entertainment fans, including classic French cuisine, Lille's distinctive culinary scene, as well as its welcoming cafés, bakeries, bars, and nightclubs.

Traditional French Cuisine

In Lille's dining scene, French cuisine—famous for its luscious tastes and superb techniques—takes center stage. The following typical French foods and specialties must be sampled while you are there:

1. **Potjevleesch** is a well-liked local cuisine that is of Flemish origin. It comprises cold, jellied meats, usually served with pig, chicken, or rabbit. The meats are cooked in a flavorful broth, and the jelly that results is then divided into pieces.

Potjevleesch is a tasty starter or main dish since it's often eaten with pickles and mustard.

2. **Carbonnade Flamande**: This hearty stew, which is created with meat, beer, and onions, is a soul-warming comfort dish. As the beef is slowly cooked, it becomes tasty and tender, and the beer gives the food a deep, malty flavor. It is often served with bread or potatoes.

3. **Endives**, or chicons as they are called in northern France, are often prepared au gratin. Endives are encased in ham, then drenched in a rich bechamel sauce and sprinkled with cheese. The meal has a delicious blend of sweet and salty tastes after baking.

4. **Waterzooi**: A common combination of veggies in waterzooi includes potatoes, leeks, carrots, and chicken or fish. "Waterzooi" means "to boil" or "to simmer," which reflects the way the meal is prepared. It captures the spirit of Flemish cuisine and is a calming and filling choice.

5. **Welsh Rarebit,** a cuisine with British roots that is popular in Lille, is a savory treat. It consists of toasted bread with a cheese sauce that often also contains beer and

mustard. For increased taste, other foods like bacon or ham are sometimes used.

Lille's Culinary Scene

Lille has a vibrant culinary culture that combines French and Flemish cuisines. There are many places to eat in the city, from little bistros to Michelin-starred establishments.

1. **Estaminet**: Northern French food may be sampled at estaminets, which are historic Flemish pubs. Local delicacies including Potjevleesch, Carbonnade Flamande, and other regional cuisines are offered at these beautiful restaurants. Estaminets provide an authentic excursion into the regional culinary tradition with their cozy, rustic environment.

2. **La Chicorée**: This Michelin-starred restaurant is renowned for its creative food, which fuses regional tastes with cutting-edge cooking methods. The restaurant offers exquisite dining with a contemporary touch via its cuisine, which features imaginative reinterpretations of local products.

3. **Le Bloempot** is a hip and hospitable eatery that has a varied cuisine made up of seasonal, fresh products. A

beautiful eating experience that emphasizes originality and quality is produced by its cuisine, which combines traditional French dishes with cutting-edge twists.

4. **Le Barbue d'Anvers**: This charming brasserie in Belgium is well-known for its mussels and beer. Several mussel recipes, such as the traditional marinière, are available, along with other shellfish and substantial Flemish cuisine.

5. **Le Comptoir Voltaire**, a cafe with a laid-back atmosphere and delectable food, is tucked away in the center of Lille. It offers well-cooked classic French cuisine including coq au vin and duck confit.

Bakeries and cafes

Coffee, pastries, and the art of unhurried living are all popular pastimes at Lille's cafés and bakeries. Here are a few you shouldn't overlook:

1. **Au Fournil de Sébastopol**: Known for its delectable pastries, bread, and cakes, this family-run bakery is a local favorite. The atmosphere at this bakery is very French, whether you're enjoying an espresso or a croissant.

2. **Méert**: A renowned pastry business known for its waffles, Méert was founded in 1761. These flavor-filled, slender, and delicate snacks are great for sweet gifts. With its opulent furnishings and displays of mouthwatering confections, the store is a visual delight in and of itself.

3. **La Patisserie Meert**: This shop is a sibling of Méert and is just as beautiful. It's the best destination to indulge in exquisitely designed sweets and macarons since it's well-known for its creative cakes and pastries.

4. **Honoré**: A beautiful café in the center of Old Lille, Honoré is the ideal place to unwind with a cup of coffee, a cup of tea, or a bottle of wine. Its inviting atmosphere and outdoor seats make it a peaceful place to people-watch.

Bars and Nightclubs

The nightlife in Lille is active and varied, with a selection of pubs and clubs to suit different interests.

Le Dandy is a classy cocktail establishment in Old Lille that's well-known for its handcrafted drinks and sophisticated ambiance. It's the perfect place to enjoy cutting-edge cocktails in a chic environment.

Le Cirque is a well-liked nightclub that incorporates a bar, restaurant, and dance floor. It's a terrific venue for those who want to dance the night away because of its vivacious environment, spacious dance floor, and wide variety of music.

Le Magazine Club is a popular venue for underground and techno music if you enjoy dance rhythms and electronic music. It's popular among those looking for cutting-edge tunes because of its vibrant atmosphere and committed clientele.

Le Bistrot de Saint-Sauveur: Le Bistrot de St So is a friendly and laid-back pub with a wide range of beers and a warm ambiance. It's the ideal location for spending a laid-back evening out with friends.

Le Mother is a popular pub and club that is well-known for its vibrant nightlife. The venue has a lively atmosphere, theme evenings, and live music. It's a great location to enjoy Lille's vibrant and varied nightlife.

Lille's dining and nightlife choices are varied and pleasant, reflecting the city's French and Flemish traditions. Lille welcomes you to immerse yourself in its rich and active culture, whether you're enjoying classic French cuisine, discovering the regional culinary scene, indulging in pastries and coffee at lovely cafes, or experiencing the energetic bars and nightclubs. So remember to appreciate the tastes and sensations that make Lille an amazing destination for food and entertainment as you stroll around the city's vibrant districts and ancient streets.

CULTURAL EXPERIENCES IN LILLE: A Tapestry of Festivals, Arts, and Traditions

Lille, a city rich in history and culture, entices visitors to explore its customs, festivals, and performing arts with its vivid tapestry of experiences. We'll examine Lille's fascinating cultural environment in this guide, emphasizing its vibrant festivals and events, flourishing theaters, and the regional traditions and customs that give the city its distinct personality.

Events and Festivals

A city that knows how to have fun is Lille. It conducts several festivals and events all year long that provide an understanding of its history, culture, and energetic environment. Some of the most prominent are listed below:

1. **The Lille Braderie** is a well-known occasion that goes back to the 12th century. It's Europe's biggest flea market, taking place the first weekend in September. Over 10,000 sellers line the streets with their wares, which include

antiques, collectibles, vintage things, and more. Music, street performances, and mouthwatering regional food, such as moules-frites (mussels and fries), all add to the joyous ambiance.

2. **The Lille Fantastic Film Festival** is an occasion that honors all things fantastic, sci-fi, and horror. It takes place in March. It gives the chance to interact with actors, directors, and other experts in the business while showcasing a wide range of films. For cinephiles and enthusiasts of the genre, the festival offers an exhilarating experience.

3. **Foire aux Manèges**: Every year in November and December, Lille hosts the Foire aux Manèges. It turns the city's core into a magical realm filled with amusement rides, contests, and sweets. Families and guests of all ages enjoy the happy atmosphere and celebrations.

4. **Lille Globe Film Festival**: This international film event, usually held in March, showcases movies from all over the globe and acts as a stage for independent and global cinema. It's a celebration of culture that introduces viewers to many viewpoints and narratives.

5. **Fête de l'Andouille**: This eccentric celebration honors andouille, a sort of smoked sausage, and is held in the adjacent town of Cambrai. Parades, music, and plenty of andouille sausages to try are all part of the occasion.

Theaters and Performing Arts

The theatrical scene in Lille is both rich and diversified, offering a variety of performances and locations to suit different creative preferences.

1. **Opéra de Lille:** The famed Opéra de Lille is a center for opera and classical music. On its calendar are orchestral events as well as performances of modern and classic operas. The opera house is a masterpiece of architecture that is renowned for its splendor and acoustics.

2. **Théâtre Sébastopol:** This old theater presents a range of entertainment, including plays, concerts, comedies, and dance recitals. It is a center for culture that offers a variety of traditional and modern shows, making sure there is something for everyone.

3. **Le Grand Sud** is a vibrant venue that features experimental theater and contemporary dance. It is

renowned for its cutting-edge and provocative performances that challenge conventional forms of art.

4. **Le Prato** is a diverse cultural institution that presents a variety of acts, including theater, dance, music, and visual arts. It serves as a center for avant-garde and experimental art, drawing artists and viewers looking for unique experiences.

5. **L'Aéronef**: Known as a nightclub and concert venue, L'Aéronef is the best spot in Lille to hear live music. It has a varied roster of musicians and bands, ranging from hip-hop and electronic to rock and pop.

Local Customs and Traditions

The distinctive local character of Lille is reflected in its customs and traditions, which represent a unique fusion of French and Flemish elements.

1. The closeness of the city to Belgium and its historical affiliation with the County of Flanders have left a strong Flemish influence on its culture. This impact is audible in regional cuisine like Potjevleesch, stepped gables in architecture, and traditional folk music.

2. **Fête de la Ducasse**: This customary Lillois celebration is observed the first weekend in September and combines religious and secular customs. Processions, parades, and the renowned Giant Parade are all part of it. These parades include colossal papier-mâché giants dressed as mythological and historical people.

3. **Carnival**: The city's carnival is a noisy event that lasts the whole month of February and features vibrant parades, mask-wearing characters, and activities. It's a time when dancing, music, and joy fill the streets of the city.

4. **Lillois Hospice Traditions** are highlighted at the Hospice Comtesse, a historic hospital that has been transformed into a museum. It sheds light on the life of the nuns who cared for the ill as well as the development of healthcare. Additionally, there are gardens on the property where medicinal herbs are grown.

5. **Lille's Dual Identity**: Lille is renowned for having a significant Flemish past in addition to being a French city. Residents take pride in this dichotomy, which is reflected in the city's customs, food, and architectural style.

Lille provides a diverse range of cultural events, whether you want to take in a theatrical production, take part in a bustling festival, or get to know the local traditions and customs. These celebrations and rituals encapsulate the city's character and history, making it a fascinating destination for those interested in learning more about its diverse cultural environment. You'll find Lille to be a city where tradition and modernity coexist, and where history is enthusiastically embraced.

OUTDOOR ADVENTURES IN LILLE: Exploring Nature and Sporting Thrills

For those seeking the beauty of nature and sports difficulties, Lille, a city that is often praised for its vibrant culture and historic charm, offers a variety of thrilling outdoor excursions. This book will go into detail on the possibilities for bicycling and hiking, day trips that take you to natural beauties, and athletic events that will make your trip to Lille exhilarating.

Biking and Hiking

Biking and hiking are great ways to enjoy the natural splendor that Lille and her surroundings have to offer. Some of the top outdoor activities in and around the city are listed below:

1. The city of Lille and its surroundings provide a choice of riding paths and routes that are appropriate for cyclists of all skill levels. The **Deûle Valley** is a well-liked option because of its lovely towpaths. These pathways, which follow the

Deûle River, offer cyclists of all skill levels a tranquil and beautiful trip. The Avenue Verte path will take you further and through more picturesque terrain to the seaside town of Bray-Dunes. To explore these beautiful paths, you may either bring your bike or hire one in Lille.

2. **Lille to the Coast**: If you're looking for a unique bike experience, think about doing the Lille to the Coast route. From Lille to the English Channel coast, you'll travel through some of northern France's most breathtaking scenery. You'll go through picturesque towns, rural areas, and even wildlife preserves. It's a wonderful chance to take in the area's varied natural splendor.

3. **Hiking in the Flanders Region:** There are several hiking routes nearby that take you through forested hills, picturesque towns, and rolling countryside. Popular hiking locations include Mont Noir, Mont Rouge, and Mont des Cats. Each path provides a chance to take in the stunning scenery and distinctive local culture of the area.

4. **Le Parc de la Deûle** is a park in Lille that offers a haven of quiet and vegetation. You may explore its riverside walking and bike routes, which provide a tranquil haven from the hustle and bustle of the city. Playgrounds, picnic

spots, and possibilities for birding are also present in the park.

Day Trips to Natural Wonders

The Lille area is a great place to start day travel since it is surrounded by stunning natural features. Here are some wonderful locations that are just a short drive away:

Less than two hours separate Lille and these famous chalk cliffs along the English Channel coast, Cap Blanc-Nez and Cap Gris-Nez. They are the ideal destination for a day trip since they provide breathtaking sea views. Hiking along the cliffs allows you to take in the stunning coastline view. The lovely beach and seafood restaurants in the neighboring village of Wissant are well-known.

Le Parc Naturel Régional Scarpe-Escaut is a local nature park that offers a tranquil natural environment and is just a short drive from Lille. It includes ponds, woodlands, and meadows and provides chances for hiking and birding. Discover the park's rich animal and plant species by hiking the park's pathways.

Les Prés du Hem is a park with magnificent lakes and lush natural areas that is close to Lille in Armentières. You may hire a paddleboat to enjoy the water, have a picnic, or take a stroll around the lakes.

Parc Mosaic is a charming day trip location in Houplin-Ancoisne, close to Lille. It is a distinctive garden park. It offers a fascinating and breathtaking experience by showcasing themed gardens and creative mosaics.

Sporting Activities

As varied as Lille's cultural offers are its athletic ones. If you like being outside, the city and its environs offer a variety of sports to get your heart racing:

1. **Canoeing and kayaking** are activities that may be done on the Deûle River and other local rivers. You may hire the necessary gear and go for a leisurely paddle along the river's lovely trails.

2. **Horseback Riding**: Several equestrian facilities in the area provide opportunities for horseback riding. Whether you're a novice or a seasoned rider, you may enjoy the

tranquil vistas while exploring the countryside on horseback.

3. **Golf**: For those who like the sport, Lille and its adjacent towns have golf courses. You may play a game of golf among stunning scenery whether you're an experienced player or a beginner who wants to give the sport a try.

4. **Rock Climbing**: Near Lille, some cliffs and quarries are ideal for rock climbing. Adventurers may climb the cliffs and rocks while surrounded by stunning scenery.

5. **Adventure Parks**: The area has adventure parks that appeal to thrill-seekers. These parks include many activities, including zip line and treetop obstacle courses.

6. **Football**: The LOSC Lille football club is based in Lille, a city with a rich athletic heritage. Football lovers may find attending a game at the Stade Pierre-Mauroy to be an exhilarating event.

Ice skating is available at the city's outdoor ice rinks if you're in Lille during the winter. In the winter months, it's an enjoyable sport for both people and families.

Lille is a popular location for outdoor enthusiasts due to the surrounding natural beauty and variety of athletic events. The area provides a broad choice of activities for people eager to appreciate the great outdoors, whether you're cycling along gorgeous roads, trekking through magnificent landscapes, or participating in exhilarating sports. Don't forget to immerse yourself in the adventure and the natural marvels that await in this exciting and colorful region of France as you visit Lille and its surroundings.

FAMILY-FRIENDLY LILLE: A Fun-Filled Adventure for All Ages

Lille, which is often praised for its rich cultural and historical legacy, is an excellent vacation spot for families. This book examines Lille's family-friendly side, showcasing kid-friendly activities, educational outings, and family-friendly restaurants that offer an enjoyable journey for all ages.

Kid-Friendly Attractions

Several family-friendly attractions in Lille are geared toward children. The following highlights will hold children's attention:

1. **The Lille Zoo (Parc Zoologique de Lille)** is a great place for families to go. It has a wide variety of creatures, including lions, giraffes, penguins, and reptiles. The purpose of the zoo is to educate visitors about animal conservation and the natural realm. For kids of all ages, it provides both an educational experience and enjoyment.

2. **La Citadelle de Lille**: La Citadelle is a medieval stronghold that is a great spot for kids to explore. There is plenty of room at the location for children to run about and explore the historic fortifications. It's a terrific location for a family picnic and for discovering the history of the city.

3. **Parc de Loisirs de la Citadelle**: This amusement park, which is close to La Citadelle, has a variety of features including a playground, a mini-golf course, and a petting zoo. Young children may have fun and enjoy outdoor activities in this wonderful location.

4. **The Lille Natural History Museum**, also known as the Musée d'Histoire Naturelle de Lille, provides young minds with an engaging experience. Natural history, biodiversity, and paleontology are the main topics of its exhibitions. Children may be in awe of animal exhibits, dinosaur fossils, and hands-on learning experiences.

5. **Wazemmes Market (Marché de Wazemmes):** The Wazemmes Market offers a bustling cultural experience as well as a place to buy. It's a great chance to expose kids to various meals, world cuisines, and the bustling market environment. Children may have a sensory journey while exploring the vibrant booths and trying local foods.

Educational Excursions

Lille offers several family-friendly educational trips that are both entertaining and enlightening. Some of the best choices are as follows:

1. **Palais des Beaux-Arts:** Families may learn a lot at Lille's Fine Arts Museum. Its vast collection comprises ornamental arts, sculptures, and paintings. The museum often conducts family-friendly events and seminars that provide youngsters with an engaging and instructive experience.

2. **Le Forum des Sciences** is an interactive scientific museum that is situated in Villeneuve-d'Ascq, a neighborhood of Lille. It is intended to awaken children's interest and love of science. Young visitors are entertained by the museum's interactive displays, planetarium programs, and workshops.

3. **LaM (Lille Métropole Museum of Modern, Contemporary, and Outsider Art)** is a museum of contemporary art that exhibits a range of creative mediums. It provides family tours and activities that give kids an exciting and easy introduction to the world of contemporary art.

4. **Musée de l'Imprimerie de Roubaix**: This printing-focused museum is situated in the adjacent town of Roubaix. It sheds light on the development of printing and its function in communication. youngsters who are interested in typography and design will find the museum to be an interesting outing since it provides educational activities for youngsters.

5. **Le LaM in Villeneuve-d'Ascq** has a special section only for kids called Le LaM - Enfants. All ages may enjoy the interactive displays and kid-friendly activities offered in this special area, which makes art and culture accessible to everyone.

Options for Family Dining

The culinary scene of Lille is not only mouth watering but also welcoming to families, offering a range of eating options:

1. **La Petite Cour**: Located close to the Palais des Beaux-Arts, La Petite Cour is a quaint and welcoming restaurant. It is a great option for families with various preferences since it provides a variety of French and foreign

meals. The courtyard setting enhances the inviting atmosphere of the eatery.

2. **Au Broc Café**: This hospitable café is close to the Lille Zoo, making it the perfect place for families to share a meal before or after going to the zoo. Sandwiches, salads, and substantial foods are all available on the menu.

3. **Le Flore:** Le Flore is a traditional French brasserie with a cuisine that appeals to a range of tastes. It's the perfect option for families that value classic French food in a laid-back setting.

4. **Les Fils à Maman** is a restaurant that youngsters will find especially fascinating because of its humorous and nostalgic appeal. It offers cuisine that makes people think of their youth, allowing for a unique and entertaining eating experience for the entire family.

5. **The Moose**: The Moose, Lille's first American sports bar, has a kid-friendly atmosphere and a menu with traditional American fare including burgers, ribs, and chicken wings. It's a wonderful location for families to experience American culture.

6. **La Pirogue**: This family-run eatery serves delectable African and Creole food and is close to the Wazemmes Market. Kids are exposed to diverse cuisines in a welcoming environment via this special culinary experience.

Lille is a great location for tourists of all ages because of its kid-friendly attractions, informative tours, and eating choices. Lille welcomes families with wide arms, whether you're taking them on informative excursions, enjoying wonderful meals, or discovering the city's cultural and historical riches. Lille is a great place for a family vacation since you can have a great time while generating lifelong memories and giving your kids meaningful experiences.

HIDDEN GEMS OF LILLE: Unveiling Off-the-Beaten-Path Treasures

Lille is often praised for its well-known landmarks and rich cultural legacy, but it also has a wealth of off-the-beaten-path treasures. We'll look at some of Lille's hidden gems in this guide and provide you with insider knowledge so you can experience the lesser-known but no less charming side of the city.

Off the Beaten path

The secret spots in Lille provide you with a distinct view of the city by escorting you away from the clamorous people to more private, calmer areas. Here are a few undiscovered highlights of Lille's charm:

1. **Rue de la Monnaie**: Many visitors often pass by this picturesque cobblestone street in Old Lille without seeing it. It is a haven for shopping looking for unusual treasures, from handmade jewelry to vintage apparel, and is lined with charming stores and artisan boutiques. Discover secret riches

by exploring the streets' underground courtyards and passageways.

2. **Le Jardin des Géants**: This little park, hidden in the middle of Lille, honors the city's giants, the enormous carnival characters known as "**les géants**." Take a stroll around the garden to appreciate these vibrant characters, each of them has a distinct personality and backstory. It's a tranquil haven that offers a window into Lille's vibrant carnival tradition.

3. **Le Pré Carré Park** is a peaceful retreat from the bustle of the city and is close to the city center. It has sculptures and other works of art, as well as a large green area where you may unwind, have a picnic, or go for a leisurely walk. The park's layout is a tasteful fusion of modern art and nature.

4. The canal that runs through Lille provides a tranquil backdrop for a leisurely bike ride or stroll. Enjoy the gorgeous surroundings as you stroll along the canal's banks and watch the boats ply the waters. It's a tranquil, less well-known spot where you may see the city differently.

5. **Rue des Bouchers**: This picturesque Vieux-Lille cobblestone road is studded with old structures that contain

a variety of stores and eateries. It's generally less congested than other of Old Lille's busier streets, and the charming and welcoming environment is ideal for a leisurely walk.

Secret Sports

The hidden areas of Lille have fascinating tales and provide one-of-a-kind experiences for those who go there. Here are a few undiscovered treasures that evoke a feeling of wonder and exploration:

1. **Villa Cavrois** is a gem of modernist architecture, and it can be found in Croix, not far from Lille. This expansive and light-filled mansion, created by architect Robert Mallet-Stevens, is a remarkable example of 20th-century architecture. With its clear lines, geometric forms, and cutting-edge design, the house provides a window into the world of modernist architecture and is available to the public.

2. **La Piscine - Musée d'Art et d'Industrie André Diligent:** The stunning La Piscine museum is located in Roubaix, a nearby city of Lille. This unusual museum has an extraordinary collection of fine art, textiles, and decorative arts and is housed in a restored swimming pool.

The breathtaking surroundings enhance the experience and foster a feeling of interest and wonder.

3. **Saint-Maurice Church**: Tourists often pass Lille's Vauban neighborhood's stunning church without seeing it. It is a hidden treasure of beauty and calm because of its exquisite stained glass windows and neo-Gothic architecture. The church is a serene location where you may look about, appreciate the architecture, or just take some time for yourself.

4. **Sébastopol Theater (Théâtre Sébastopol):** For those who value the arts, this old theater is a hidden treasure. Although it's not a typical tourist destination, you may see a range of acts there, such as plays, concerts, and dance performances. The cozy atmosphere of the theater makes for a more intimate and immersive experience.

5. **Porte de Paris:** The entry to Lille's Old Town is marked by this less well-known city gate. With its neoclassical style and elaborate ornamentation, it is a work of architectural art. It may not be as well-known as some of Lille's other attractions, but history and architectural buffs should check it out.

Local Insights

It's vital to obtain knowledge from residents who are familiar with the city's secrets if you want to properly appreciate Lille's hidden beauties. Here are some advice and suggestions for the area:

Many of Lille's ancient buildings include secret courtyards that are not visible from the street. These courtyards often conceal unexpected features like quaint cafés, stores, or art pieces. Locals are aware that spending some time exploring these tunnels might result in exciting discoveries.

Lille is well-known for its flea markets and brocantes, which often take place in different areas. Locals go to these events often in search of rare antiques, vintage goods, and treasures. Make sure to check the calendar of nearby events to see if one falls during your stay.

The Wonders of Regional Cuisine: While Lille's regional cuisines are well-praised, the city's culinary scene also has some hidden jewels. To experience true regional cuisines, locals advise checking out lesser-known restaurants and cafés. Asking for suggestions can help you find the best places in your area.

The Craft Beer Scene in Lille: Beer lovers should investigate the expanding craft beer scene in Lille. A variety of handcrafted beers that highlight the ingenuity and passion of local brewers are available at hidden microbreweries and taprooms. Trying these beers offers a distinctive glimpse into Lille's contemporary culture.

Street Art and the Arts: Lille has a flourishing art community. Locals advise spending some time exploring the murals and other urban art pieces throughout the city. Numerous areas are home to these undiscovered works of art, which give the city an additional touch of creative appeal.

The opportunity to dive deeper into Lille's culture, history, and everyday life is provided by its hidden jewels. You may learn the secrets that make Lille a city of surprising discoveries by exploring these off-the-beaten-path marvels. You'll discover a Lille that is rich in history, art, and the genuine experiences that inhabitants value when you explore beyond the well-known landmarks.

DAY TRIPS FROM LILLE: Exploring Bruges, Arras and Vimy Ridge, and the Opal Coast

Lille, a fascinating city in and of itself, acts as a starting point for a variety of amazing day trip locations. These day tours provide a variety of experiences that might improve your journey to the area, from the enchanted appeal of Bruges in Belgium to the historical importance of Arras and Vimy Ridge and the tranquil beauty of the beaches along the Opal Coast.

1) Belgium's Bruges: An Epic Escape

Approximately 80 kilometers (50 miles) separate Lille.

Travel time is around one hour by car or one and a half hours by rail.

Why Visit Bruges

The lovely medieval city of Bruges, sometimes known as the "**Venice of the North**," seems to have stood still through the ages. It has picturesque canals, cobblestone streets, and well-preserved buildings. An idyllic retreat from the busy metropolis, a day trip to Bruges from Lille is like entering a storybook.

What to See and Do

The center of Bruges is the **Markt Square (Grote Markt)**, which is flanked by spectacular buildings including the Provincial Court and the Belfry Tower.

Climb the Belfry of Bruges' 366 stairs for sweeping views of the city. It is recognized as a **Bruges landmark.**

Canal Tour: Take a canal tour to see Bruges from a new angle. You'll see magnificent bridges, historic structures, and lovely gardens.

Wander around the calm Beguinage **(Begijnhof)** in Bruges to see the white-painted homes. The beguines, a laity religious group, previously called it home.

Visit the **windmills** outside of the city of Bruges for beautiful vistas and a look into conventional Dutch construction.

2) A Historical Journey Between Arras and Vimy Ridge

Nearly 45 kilometers (28 miles) separate Lille from Arras, while 65 kilometers (40 miles) separate Lille from Vimy Ridge.

Travel Time: 30 to 40 minutes by rail to Arras, and another 30 minutes by automobile to Vimy Ridge

Why Visit Vimy Ridge and Arras?

A distinctive day excursion from Lille is available to Arras, a lovely town with well-preserved architecture, and Vimy Ridge. The trek sheds light on the First World War's history and the region's resiliency.

What to See and Do in Arras

The Place des Héros, the heart of Arras, is surrounded by stunning structures in the Flemish Baroque style. It's a fantastic location for eating and drinking.

Climb the Arras Belfry (**Beffroi d'Arras**) for sweeping vistas of the city. An interesting trip may be taken into the belfry's subterranean passageways.

Discover the **Les Boves** in Arras, which were originally chalk quarries and provide a unique viewpoint on the history of the city.

What to See and Do at Ridge

The famous monument known as the Canadian National Vimy Memorial honors the Canadian troops who fought in the Battle of Vimy Ridge during World War I. The website provides a moving and stirring experience.

Guided tours of the surviving trenches and tunnels at Vimy Ridge provide visitors with an understanding of the circumstances and experiences of the troops throughout the conflict.

3) The Opal Coast's Beaches: A Coastal Getaway

Distances from Lille to other communities along the Opal Coast range.

Approximately one to one and a half hours by vehicle

Why Visit Opal Coast

The Opal Coast is a pleasant getaway from the city with its immaculate beaches, breathtaking cliffs, and beautiful coastal villages. Numerous seaside locations are available, each with its personality.

What to Do and See

Wimereux has a long, sandy beach that is ideal for taking a leisurely walk. It is a charming coastal village. The town's architecture has a Belle Époque feel to it.

These stunning chalk cliffs, known as **Cap Gris-Nez and Cap Blanc-Nez,** provide amazing views of the English Channel. It's the perfect location for trekking and seeing the coastline.

Le Touquet-Paris-Plage: Also known as Le Touquet, this town has a buzzing beach vibe. Enjoy the sandy beach, look around fashionable shops, and eat seafood at nearby restaurants.

Ambleteuse: Fort Mahon, a fort from the 17th century that has been carefully conserved, is located here, making it a worthwhile historical stop along the Opal Coast.

Visit Boulogne-sur-Mer's historic center, meander around the city walls, and see Nausicaá, one of Europe's biggest aquariums.

Tips for your Day Trips

Travel Options: Take into account your chosen means of transportation when organizing your day travels. While a vehicle offers flexibility and access to more distant regions, trains are a handy solution for certain journeys.

Local food: While on your day trips, don't pass up the chance to sample local food. Enjoy handcrafted treats, seafood, and regional delicacies.

Guided Tours: Some historical locations, like Vimy Ridge, provide guided tours to help you better comprehend the importance of the place.

Considerations for the Seasons: When organizing your day travels, keep in mind the seasonal fluctuations. For instance, the Opal Coast is quite attractive in the summer, while Bruges may be charming with its Christmas lights in the winter.

Timing: If you want to get the most out of a visit to a particular place, you should plan your day travels around the opening and closing times.

From the historical importance of Arras and Vimy Ridge to the maritime splendor of the beaches along the Opal Coast, day excursions from Lille offer a variety of experiences. These locations enhance your trip to the area by enabling you to discover a variety of topographies, civilizations, and historical accounts. Lille is the ideal starting place for amazing day adventures, whether your interests are peace, history, or the allure of the sea.

PRACTICAL INFORMATION FOR YOUR LILLE ADVENTURE

To ensure a smooth and pleasurable stay, it is essential to have useful information at your fingertips as you plan your trip to Lille. To assist you in navigating your Lille experience with ease, this book offers essential information on language and communication, safety and health, local laws and traditions, helpful websites and apps, travel agencies, major destinations and landmarks, and some handy French words and expressions.

Health and Safety

Generally speaking, Lille is a safe city for visitors, but it's always vital to use common sense caution. Here are some health and safety advice:

Emergency Numbers: 112 is the standard emergency number in Europe. Dial 15 to reach medical help. Call the police at (17). Dial 18 to reach the fire department.

Healthcare: The healthcare system of Lille is well advanced. The majority of medical treatments should be covered for travelers from Europe who have an EHIC. Travelers from outside of Europe should have travel insurance that includes medical coverage.

Immunizations: Before coming to Lille or France, confirm with your local health authorities if any vaccines are advised or necessary.

Pickpocketing: Be aware of pickpockets in busy places, particularly at tourist attractions and on public transit, as you would in any city. Keep your possessions safe.

Walking at Night: Lille is typically safe at night, but proceeds with care and stays in busy, well-lit areas.

Traffic Safety: If you want to drive or use public transit, be aware of the rules regarding parking and traffic. Be cautious while crossing roads in France since French drivers may be aggressive.

Local Laws and Customs

For a courteous and trouble-free stay in Lille, it is essential to understand local rules and customs:

Smoking: Smoking is not permitted in any indoor public area, including pubs, restaurants, and transit.

Service charges are already included in restaurant pricing. To round up the sum or leave tiny change as a tip, nevertheless, is usual. Locals often leave spare change at cafés or round up the amount.

Alcohol: The French legal drinking age is 18. There is no shortage of alcohol, and French wine is highly regarded. However, intoxication in public and disorderly conduct are not encouraged.

Dress Code: When visiting religious places, dress neatly and modestly. Although Lille is a contemporary city, it is nevertheless customary to cover your shoulders and knees when going inside cathedrals or churches.

Public Conduct: Lille citizens admire decency and kindness. The common consensus is that loud talks or disruptive conduct in public areas are not acceptable, and public shows of love should be kept to a minimum.

The majority of Lille's stores and markets are open from 9:00 AM to 7:00 PM, including an hour for lunch. In the afternoon, many small businesses could shut for a few hours. Many stores are closed or just open for a short time on Sundays.

Useful Websites and Apps

Lille has several websites and mobile applications that might improve your trip:

The official website for Lille tourism, **lilletourism.com**, offers information on attractions, events, lodgings, and more.

The official mobile app for public transit in Lille and the surrounding area is called **RATP**. It provides choices for buying tickets as well as maps and schedules.

The **V'Lille app** aids in finding available bikes and docking stations if you want to utilize the city's bike-sharing program.

Maps on Google Google Maps is a flexible navigational tool that is especially helpful for locating nearby attractions, eateries, and public transit alternatives.

Duolingo: The Duolingo app provides interactive language classes if you're looking to brush up on your French language abilities.

TripAdvisor: This app is useful for finding reviews and suggestions for Lille hotels, restaurants, and sights.

Travel Agencies

Even while many people love making their travel plans, other people may prefer the help of a travel agency, particularly for complicated excursions or guided tours. These are some of the travel businesses in Lille:

Offering a range of travel packages, such as tours, cruises, and all-inclusive getaways, is **Voyages FRAM**.

Thomas Cook is a well-known travel company that offers a variety of alternatives to customers.

Leclerc Voyages is a member of the E. Leclerc grocery chain that offers affordable travel arrangements and services.

Look Voyages: renowned for its travels to far-off places.

Decathlon Voyages offers a variety of outdoor activities and specializes in sports and adventure travel.

Key Locations and Landmarks

Your visit to Lille may be improved by being familiar with important places and landmarks:

Grand Place: The heart of Old Lille, encircled by stunning Flemish design.

La Vieille Bourse is a historic structure with a charming courtyard that often hosts chess tournaments and book sales.

The Fine Arts Museum of Lille, known for its vast art collection, is called the **Palais des Beaux-Arts.**

Lille Zoo is a fun family destination with a wide range of animals and beautifully planted settings.

The beautiful, modern **Cathédrale Notre-Dame de la Treille** has a distinctive architectural style.

The Lille Opera House is well-known for both its magnificent exterior and its extensive schedule of events.

A tranquil park featuring walking trails, a zoo, and a playground next to La Citadelle is called **Parc de la Citadelle.**

Hector Guimard created the stunning Art Nouveau home known as **Maison Coilliot.**

The LaM (Lille Métropole Museum of Contemporary, Contemporary, and Outsider Art) is a museum dedicated to contemporary art that features a variety of well-known and up-and-coming artists.

During your visit to Lille, these landmarks will serve as interesting attractions and helpful guiding points.

French Expressions and Phrases
Although English is widely spoken in Lille, you can engage with locals more effectively if you know a few basic French words. Here are some typical sayings and expressions:

Bonjour (bohn-zhoor): Hello
Bonsoir (bohn-swahr) Good evening
S' ll vous plaît (seel voo pleh): Please
Merci (mehr-see): thank you
Oui (wee) Yes
Non (noh) No
Parlez- vous anglais? (par leh vooz ahn leh?) Do you speak English?
L' addition, s'll vous plaît (la-dee-syon, seel voo pleh): The bills, please

The locals will enjoy your use of these words and your kind manner, which may result in fruitful conversations.

Having this useful information on hand for your trip to Lille will ensure that you are well-prepared to make the most of your stay. You'll have the skills you need to have a seamless and enjoyable trip in this attractive French city, from knowing the traditions and regulations of the area to communicating and navigating the city successfully.

LILLE ON A BUDGET: Exploring the City Without Breaking the Bank

Budgeting for a trip to Lille is not only feasible but also a worthwhile experience. This vivacious French city has a large selection of free and inexpensive activities, reasonably priced dining alternatives, and cost-effective lodging options. Whether you're a student, backpacker, or just a budget tourist, this guide will show you how to get the most out of your time in Lille without breaking the bank.

Free and Low-Cost Attractions

The history, culture, and beauty of Lille may be experienced without breaking the bank thanks to the city's wealth of free and reasonably priced attractions. The following locations and activities are must-dos:

Grand Place & Old Lille: Take a stroll around Old Lille's quaint cobblestone streets and take in the breathtaking Flemish architecture. A major plaza where you may enjoy the beautiful surroundings is called Grand Place.

On the first Sunday of every month, admittance to the **Palais des Beaux-Arts** is free, despite the permanent collection of the museum requiring a ticket. This is a fantastic chance to see a top-notch art collection without spending any money.

Parc de la Citadelle: Enjoy a stroll or a picnic in this huge park. You may stroll around the lovely gardens, see the zoo, and take in the serene atmosphere.

Le Jardin des Géants: This little garden honors Lille's carnival giants and is located in the city's center. You may find out all about the local carnival tradition at this special free attraction.

Street Art & Murals: The street art movement in Lille is growing, and the city is covered with vibrant murals and graffiti. It's a cost-free and creative approach to learning about Lille's contemporary culture.

Old Lille's Rue de la Monnaie is packed with artisan stores and boutiques. While purchasing here might be pricey, admiring the artistry of regional goods is free and can be done from afar.

Explore the castle in the form of a star that was built by the military engineer Vauban. The UNESCO World Heritage Site of the Citadel provides historical context.

Affordable Eateries

For tourists on a tight budget, Lille's culinary scene is a treat since it provides a variety of inexpensive eating alternatives without sacrificing quality. Here are some locations where you may enjoy regional tastes without going broke:

Estaminet: Lille is well known for its estaminets, which are classic French pubs. Experience genuine and reasonably priced local cuisine at an estaminet by indulging in delicacies like potjevleesch (meat terrine) and carbonnade flamande (beef stew).

Visit the bustling Wazemmes Market (**Marché de Wazemmes**) to experience a range of regional delicacies including cheese, charcuterie, and fresh fruit. With your market findings, you can put together an affordable picnic.

Friterie: Friteries are the greatest venues to taste the fries that Lille is famous for. Get a cone of fries and a selection of sauces. It is a fast and reasonably priced snack.

Boulangeries: A variety of tasty and fresh selections are available in Lille's bakeries. Simple baguette sandwiches and pastries may be enjoyed without breaking the bank.

Cafés and Brasseries: Nearby cafés and brasseries often provide inexpensive set lunch menus (menu du jour) and daily specials. These meals often cost less than $10 and provide an appetizer, a main course, and a dessert.

Small Markets: You may get inexpensive street food and refreshments at several other small markets in Lille in addition to Wazemmes Market.

Budget-Friendly Accommodation

For tourists on a tight budget, Lille offers a variety of lodging alternatives, including guesthouses, hostels, and low-cost hotels. Here are a few suggestions:

Hostels: Many hostels in Lille provide reasonably priced dorm-style rooms and common areas. St. Christopher's Inn Hostel and Gastama Hostel are a few more well-liked choices.

Budget Hotels: Several hotels in Lille are reasonably priced and provide basic facilities as well as pleasant rooms. Hotel Continental, Hotel Flandre Angleterre, and Hotel Saint Maurice are a few examples.

Guesthouses: Staying at a guesthouse may be less expensive and more individualized. For a taste of the neighborhood, look for guesthouses in residential districts.

Apartment Rentals: There are several reasonably priced apartment rentals available in Lille on websites like Airbnb and Vrbo. For tourists who value a comfortable setting and the freedom to prepare their meals, this choice is great.

Camping: If you like the outdoors, think about camping alternatives close to Lille. Several campsites provide inexpensive lodging for campers.

Utilize last-minute booking websites and applications to discover lower costs of hotels and lodging in Lille.

Youth Hostels: Lille has several hostels for young people and travelers. These hostels provide a communal setting and are often inexpensive.

Budget Travel Tips

Use Public Transportation: The public transportation system in Lille is effective and reasonably priced. For discounts on several travels, take into account buying a transportation pass.

Take advantage of **free museum days** by visiting places like the Palais des Beaux-Arts, which is open for free on the first Sunday of every month.

Picnicking: Have inexpensive meals by taking a picnic in a park-like Parc de la Citadelle or Jardin des Géants.

Visit Local Markets: Look around your neighborhood for fresh vegetables, cheeses, and snacks that are reasonably priced.

Lunch Menus: Lunch is a wonderful time to eat out since so many restaurants provide fixed lunch menus that are reasonably priced.

Look into any city passes that give savings on activities and transit that are available in Lille.

Student discounts should always be requested at museums and other attractions if you're a student.

Budgeting for a trip to Lille is not only feasible but also a rewarding experience. Lille has a wealth of opportunities to experience the city without breaking the bank, from free and inexpensive activities to reasonable cafes and cost-effective lodging. You can enjoy Lille's top attractions while keeping your costs under control with some clever preparation and a spirit of adventure.

SAMPLE ITINERARY: A Festive Winter Getaway in Lille

Lille is the ideal location for a joyous winter trip because of its alluring beauty and contagious Christmas enthusiasm. This example schedule will lead you through a great vacation experience in Lille, from discovering the Christmas markets to enjoying classic French food.

Arrival at the Lille Christmas Market on Day 1

Morning
When you get to Lille, check into your hotel. During the Christmas season, a lot of hotels and guesthouses are exquisitely adorned, creating a comfortable atmosphere.

For a classic French breakfast of croissants, pain au chocolat, and café au lait, visit a nearby café.

Afternoon
Start your holiday journey by visiting the Place Rihour Christmas market, which is the focal point of Lille's seasonal festivities. Discover the market's wooden chalets, which are

lit up with dazzling lights, and look around for one-of-a-kind presents, seasonal delicacies, and crafts.

A wonderful gaufre **(waffle)** or warm, roasted chestnuts from the market booths are not to be missed.

Evening
Enjoy a spectacular experience as the sun sets by exploring the city's lit streets. An inviting and happy mood is created by the holiday lighting and decorations.

Dine out for supper at a neighborhood spot renowned for its seasonal fare. Try local favorites like coq au vin or duck confit, then end your lunch with a delicious crème brûlée.

Day 2: Exploring Lille's Sights

Morning
One of France's biggest museums of fine arts is the Palais des Beaux-Arts, where you should start your day. Admire the remarkable collection of artwork, which includes pieces by well-known artists.

Choose a meal at a neighborhood brasserie for lunch so you may have a substantial pot-au-feu (boiled beef) or seafood dish with a glass of French wine.

Afternoon
Wander around Old Lille at your leisure, taking in the quaint architecture and discovering the boutiques and artisan stores. Find special presents or mementos to help you remember your vacation.

Visit the Vieille Bourse, the historic stock exchange, to see the book markets and possibly even local chess.

Evening
Make your way to the Lille Christmas Market as night falls to take in the illuminations and the joyous ambiance.

A traditional tavern where you can enjoy local fares like potjevleesch and carbonnade flamande while drinking local beer might be a pleasant place to have dinner.

Day 3: a day trip to Belgium's Bruges

Morning

Set off on a thrilling day excursion to Belgium's Bruges. During the Christmas season, the fantasy village is turned into a wintry wonderland.

Visit the city's main Christmas market in Bruges. Examine the vendors, indulge in some mulled wine, and take in the holiday accents.

Afternoon

Discover the charming canals and medieval buildings of Bruges' old city center, a UNESCO World Heritage Site.

Don't pass up the chance to indulge in Belgian treats like beer, chocolate, and waffles.

Evening

In the evening, go back to Lille and take pleasure in a peaceful meal there. During the Christmas season, a lot of neighborhood eateries provide festive cuisine and seasonal menus.

Continuation and Departure on Day 4

Morning

Take part in a gastronomic journey on your last day in Lille. Participate in a culinary class to learn how to make classic French holiday foods. You may make your own bûche de Noël (**Christmas log cake)** or other seasonal sweets.

Celebrate your newly acquired culinary talents while enjoying the fruits of your cooking lesson at lunch.

Afternoon
Investigate any shops or sights you may have missed in the afternoon. Don't forget to stop by the Christmas market to pick up any last-minute presents and goodies for the season.

If you have time, go for a stroll in one of Lille's picturesque parks or gardens to take in the brisk winter air.

Evening
Finish your journey with a celebratory meal in a welcoming restaurant. You may choose from a special festive menu or traditional French fare like boeuf Bourguignon.

After dinner, take one more leisurely walk around the elegantly lighted streets to take in the magical festive ambiance.

FESTIVE RECIPES: Cooking Up Christmas Delights

Here are two classic dishes to recreate the joyous tastes of Lille at home:

1) The traditional French meal **coq au vin** is excellent for holiday celebrations. It's a substantial and filling dish made with chicken, red wine, mushrooms, and fragrant herbs. Serve it with crispy French toast or creamy mashed potatoes.

Ingredients

1 whole chicken, divided into parts
750 ml of red wine, ideally Burgundy
150g diced bacon
Small pearl onions, 250g
250g sliced mushrooms, 2 cloves minced garlic
All-purpose flour, 2 tablespoons
2 tbsp. of butter
2/TBS of olive oil
Bouquet garni (parsley, thyme, and bay leaf)
pepper and salt as desired

Instructions

For at least six hours or overnight, marinate the chicken pieces in red wine with the bouquet garni.

Cook the chicken pieces in hot olive oil in a big skillet. Take out and put aside.

Add the bacon, onions, and mushrooms to the same skillet. Brown food in the oven.

Cook for a few minutes after adding the flour to the mixture.

Add the minced garlic and return the chicken to the pan along with the wine used for marinating.

The chicken should be tender after 1.5 to 2 hours of simmering over low heat.

To taste, add salt and pepper to the food.

Enjoy the taste of Lille when serving hot.

2) Christmas cake (Yule log cake)

During the Christmas season, many people eat the classic French dessert known as **bûche de noel**. It's a cheerful, eye-catching confection that resembles a yule log. This is how you create one:

Ingredients

(Homemade or store-bought) sponge cake
Ganache or chocolate buttercream
Meringue mushrooms, used as ornaments
powdered cocoa (for dusting)

Instructions

A chocolate or vanilla sponge cake should be baked or purchased and allowed to cool.

Over the cake, spread a layer of chocolate buttercream or ganache.

Starting at one end, form the cake into a log. To make it seem like a branch, cut a diagonal slice from one end and connect it to the side.

More chocolate buttercream or ganache should be applied on top of the cake to give it a bark-like texture.

For a realistic look, garnish with meringue mushrooms and dusted with cocoa powder.

Cut this delicious Christmas dessert into slices and serve.

By using these recipes, you may enjoy the festive tastes all year long while bringing a bit of Lille's Christmas season into your own home. Good appetite!

CONCLUSION

A trip to Lille provides a beautiful fusion of history, culture, and festive charm, making it a desirable location all year round. Lille has everything to offer any tourist, from the charming Christmas markets to the fascinating museums and great dining experiences. The city's distinctive identity distinguishes it from other French cities due to its distinctive fusion of French and Flemish elements.

The draw of Lille is apparent, whether you're strolling through the cobblestone alleys of Old Lille, sampling the local cuisine, or taking day excursions to surrounding attractions like Bruges or Arras. The city offers a warm and welcoming environment that makes every tourist feel at home and welcomes them with open arms.

As you make plans for your trip to Lille, keep in mind that the city is more than simply a place to visit; it's a journey full of memorable cultural experiences, delectable culinary delights, and celebratory occasions. So, enjoy Lille's allure and engross yourself in the captivating French gem's rich tapestry.

TOP 10 MUST-VISIT CHRISTMAS ATTRACTIONS IN LILLE

Christmas Markets: The markets in Lille are renowned. Visit the colorful wooden chalets at Place Rihour, which feature one-of-a-kind items for sale, crafts, and delicious food. Don't overlook the enormous Ferris wheel and sparkling lights at the Grand Place market.

Parc de la Citadelle's Winter Wonderland: During the Christmas season, Parc de la Citadelle is transformed into a fantastical winter wonderland. There is a skating rink, a Christmas market, and lovely lights around the park. Fantastic for family trips.

The Marché de Wazemmes is a bustling market filled with festive treats. Shop for seasonal gifts, gourmet foods, and fresh fruit. Enjoy the lively ambiance and delight in regional cuisine.

Cathédrale Notre-Dame de la Treille: During the Christmas season, this modern cathedral is exquisitely lit. Attend a joyful service, take in the stunning architecture, and experience the Christmas spirit that permeates its interiors.

Visit the Vauban Citadel, a UNESCO World Heritage Site, to get a taste of history and festive beauty. You may wander the fortress's grounds and take in breathtaking city views when it is lit up.

Take a leisurely evening walk through **Lille's lit streets** on the Christmas Lights Walk. Sparkling lights cover the city, transforming it into a lovely setting ideal for a romantic getaway or a family excursion.

Discover a special garden honoring the giants of Lille's carnival tradition at **Le Jardin des Géants**. The garden offers access to local customs and is free to visit.

The Lille Christmas Parade is a joyous yearly event that features merry floats, upbeat music, and jovial entertainers. The parade is a must-see event throughout Lille's festive season.

Ice skating at Place de la République: Place de la République is a thrilling ice skating location in the center of

Lille. The rink is a great location to enjoy the festive spirit and make priceless memories.

Christmas concerts and shows are presented throughout the year at Lille's theaters and music venues. Discover the musical aspect of the season by listening to anything from village choirs to major orchestras.

The top 10 Christmas attractions in Lille guarantee a merry and fantastic day that will fill your heart with joy and leave you with priceless holiday memories. Lille's Christmas spirit is certain to capture your attention whether you're looking for one-of-a-kind presents, indulging in seasonal sweets, or just taking in the city's brilliant lights.

(HAPPY TRAVELS)

Printed in Great Britain
by Amazon